Three Men

*Andy Croft, W. N. Herbert
and Paul Summers*

Five Leaves Publications
www.fiveleaves.co.uk

Three Men on the Metro

by Andy Croft, W.N. Herbert and Paul Summers

Published in 2009 by Five Leaves Publications,
PO Box 8786, Nottingham NG1 9AW
www.fiveleaves.co.uk

ISBN: 978 1 905512 84 3

Copyright © Andy Croft, W. N. Herbert and Paul Summers, 2009

Five Leaves acknowledges financial support from
Arts Council England

Five Leaves is represented to the trade by Turnaround and distributed by
Central Books.
We are members of Inpress (www.inpressbooks.co.uk)

Cover design: Four Sheets Design and Print
Typesetting and layout: Parker & Collinson Ltd
Printed by Imprint Digital in the UK

'To Moscow! To Moscow! To Moscow!'
(Anton Chekhov, *The Three Sisters*)

'Well, how is the Metro?'
(Osip Mandelstam)

'There is no shame in not knowing; the shame lies in not finding out.'
(Russian proverb)

'Beneath Moscow
Comrade Mole
Has opened its mouth
Really wide.'
(Vladimir Mayakovsky)

'Long live the underground!'
(Fyodor Dostoevsky)

'There will be no useful information in this book.'
(Jerome K. Jerome, *Three Men on the Bummel*)

For Vera

Acknowledgements

Thanks are due to the Arts Council of England for supporting this project. We also owe thanks to Rachael Ogden, Kate Griffin and Claire Malcolm for helping us get to Moscow, and to Tom Birchenough, Sonya Ter-Avakova, Tanya Ilyina and Sasha Semenyuk for looking after us while we were there. Thanks also to Konstantin Cherkasskiy for showing us around the Moscow Metro Museum, to James Meek, Alexis Dushkin, Dima Topolski, Alexandra Paperno and Galina Lushnikovsa for advice, help and warmth, and to OGI for the soup, fried eggs, coffee, beer and ashtrays.

CONTENTS

The authors are identified following their poems as follows: *ЭК* = AC (Andy Croft); *ВНХ* = WNH (Bill Herbert); *ПС* = PS (Paul Summers)

Prologue: Monumentski, Haymarketiy, Centralskaya

Now that we're back I find me
                              looking differently up
the escalator's rattle of a trachea,
                              strict-angled to the cars,
like a torch-lit snorkel's innard
                    leaning towards air
still staring up-
            ward from Plutonian layers,
from the buried palaces, mansions in the muck,
clay-encased chateaux of Chistiye Stalin dead
Krushkiev dead
                KrasnoBrezhnev dead
                              Arbatropov dead
GorbachoProkoPrufrockiev
                    heard
the chorus of drowned Komsomols,
the worksongs of our Comrade Moles,
the Tsar's Volgaic gnomes
all singing the attributes of Lenin's dynasty
'Ba-ald hair bald
              ba-ald hair bald'
Then Yeltsin, Putin, Medvedev, embalming themselves
in the honey of power, cutting their own flanks
with an disinterred, disinterested sickle
and pouring vodka in their veins,
borscht into their arteries.
I feel them rank behind me
                    the cep-helmeted dead
of Smolenskaya, the *greeb*-Ghiberti everywhere
celebrated as they were being butchered,
champignon cast plaster
                    painted bronze in Baumanskaya,

all boletus-medallioned and Della Robbiad,
gill-ribbed in Taganskaya, frieze-dried to the walls
like ancient keich,
                    cow-dung spattered among
the golden corn in Kurskaya, that Stalin touched
and turned
            to corpse, to copper,
                                to heavy bread of brass
in the buried jawbone of the Ukrainean Thirties
in the transported fontanelle of the Georgian forties
in the eliminated pelvis of the Jewish fifties.

So looking up from our would-be deeper stations,
well-strip-lit against the weight of little dark,
you know this must begin by looking back,
that yielding of Eurydice
                        the instant that he knew
nothing walks behind you;
                            how the dead have left
identity behind
                and fill us with its lack:
he heard
        how nothing walks,
                            its footsteps' slap;
knew how the soul, abandoned, must become
the self abandoning, doubled up and emptying
till Orpheus becomes
                    past Orpheus
or hope of whole conviction;
                            he lost love's grip on us
as though it is the other; knowing this
the song that makes the rocks despair, he despaired –
since Maenads are murderously sane
and sameness tears us rights from righteousness,
the prospect of their mirror's like the grave; he saw how
you see yourself, turning at the tunnel's mouth

letting go of that last century's young
I know these are the only first words
of the song I can't remember, sung
as they pass me by, diluvial shades,
entering the sketched-out caves, picking up
the barest tools beside the scratched-out rail
they haven't lain yet, starting to chip
and hack at the sweating flanks of clay,
the soiled and solid stone so each stroke tears,
staccato-Stakhanovite, a passage through
their own flesh, each blow's a line
laid down their breastbones, so,
breathing in the watered faith,
they're gouging up their own fresh spines.

greeb (гриб) — mushroom

BHX

Metronomic

In the morning I go down in the Metro
There my underground life runs away.
(Valery Syutkin)

Three hundred feet below the ground,
The Circle Line goes round and round,
De-clunk de-da, de-clunk de-da,
Four syllables to every bar.
'Dear Passengers,' the tannoy says,
Uncomradely, though polished phrase
In regular paeonic feet
That fits the Metro rush-hour beat
Of workers paid to feed machines.
The male voice on the tannoy means
We're ticking clockwise round the stain
Of Stalin's coffee cup again;
An urgent metre, keeping time,
To which we nod our heads in rhyme
And mark the stress for emphasis,
Rabotniks from *Metropolis*,
Or clockwork soldiers on parade;
A rhythm made to be obeyed
By veterans with medalled chests,
And Moscow girls with perfect breasts,
And Moscow girls with almond eyes,
And businessmen in suits and ties,
And college kids who text and text
Between one station and the next:
I'm on the train, I'm on the train
I'm on the train, I'm on the train…

ЭК

the beautiful lie

beneath a vaulted arch that's washed
with lime, the flaking skin of passing
time reveals old joe caught in repose.
when the earth is damp & the mould
blooms ripe, a smoking gun appears, an
unlit pipe conjoining with his roaming,
georgian nose, & not unlike pinocchio's,
they say it grows with every pretty lie

we hear or tell, with every leap of faith
we make & every unheard prayer, each
sweet mistake, each conjured hell; it
grows like cancer's cold farewell, the only
spell to counter it the hopeful beat, the
fragile swell of every newborn's fontanel.

ПС

Notes from the Undermind 1

Time and the Metro love directing
their passengers towards those goals
each thinks is his. No good perfecting
your tunnelled life, good Comrade Mole,
if where your present, past and future
get linked in triple-knotted suture
is also known as, well, the grave,
and no more point in being brave
or sober, son - get stewed, go canine;
sing in the *banyas*, chase the ZiLs;
denounce your neighbour, neck your pills –
anything but roll round this trainline
dream in, regime out, till you die...
and then you notice: time's a lie.

The Metro's icons, too, deceived us:
its paradise looked down, aghast,
as sheaves of shells, not corn, bereaved us
of hope: all harvests turned at last
to that reward of shit-scared squaddies:
barns filled with rapes, mills choked with bodies –
a surplus that wiped values out,
the Motherland washed clean in gouts
of any blood, kulaks' or killers',
Chechyen or Georgian, Jew or Pole,
Germans galore, jammed in Death's hole...
and Russians - always good for filler –
Russians, like kasha, gruel or bread,
Russians will always round out the dead.

Everything we place beneath is lost or
skeletal ideology –
only the Metro keeps its lustre,
by swallowing itself it says
'Forget words' surface, vote for vowels –
all palaces are in your bowels.'
Ideologues cannot forgive
beneath belief is where we live
with mole and mandrake, salamander –
no apparachnik, no mad priest
can keep all underpants policed;
no desktop-pounding Alexander
can turn a theory into joy:
beneath belief's another Troy.

banya (баня) — bathhouse

BHX

Notes from the Undermind 2

Near May Day on the Sparrow Hills
it's time to mash the ages, churn
the Metro's myths with H.G.Wells,
like Pushkin mished till kin with Burns;
then add Jerome, his jug-head trio,
and Fyodor, for fevered brio –
till Moscow sees a Sphinx's mouth,
cloacal, O-shaped, blaring out
this bummer of a song, that progress
is just a train, sent underground,
its won't-stay-buried shrieking sound
the mating cry of some mad ogress
or else her baby, needing fed
a bloody star in human bread.

Since Metro's from the Greek for 'mother',
something fallopian's in the Tube:
each city egging on each other,
to build Dystopia in its pubes.
Therefore three rubes went on the bummel
and scavenged verse in every tunnel
each *stantsia* a stanza, till
their book of rails had drunk its fill
of chandelier, mosaic and marble,
stained glass and swag and bas-relief:
all those imperial motifs
that make a very Marxist garble,
where cornfield and cannon still contest
their place at Mother Russia's breast.

stantsia (станция) — station

BHX

The Dog's Bollocks

Though cowards flinch and traitors snigger,
We cannot help but stand and stare
Before each touching, crouching figure
Deep down in Revolution Square.
Who could not love such noble creatures?
Their kindly but heroic features
Suggest a race of Myrmidons,
The rational Future cast in bronze.
For luck - or else to ward off failure –
Commuters rub the guard-dog's nose,
Till you could even say it glows;
They also stroked its genitalia
But higher organs disapproved
And now he's had his balls removed.

ЭК

Ploshad' Revolyutsiy

That in this crouching, crimson palace,
supported by dark, shouldered bronze,
the Revolution bares its phallus
displays how sexy it felt – once.
Who couldn't know that, fondly handled,
proud bronze comes to a flame, like candles?
So it's no accident this hall
is strewn with stick-bombs and dogs' balls,
huge drills and pert, long-barrelled pistols –
and all this twice, so Moscow flocks
through a happy station with two cocks.
Just so the Church marked her apostles
with cockerel, keys, and fingers' thrust:
belief digs deepest, spurred by lust.

BHX

ghosts

the boy in the denim suit
gnaws on his knuckles
each chubby digit glazed
with spittle. his grandma
looks like brezhnev
grey and unmoved,
the camber of her sepia eyes
preoccupied with losses.

& sasha *mechtatel* mourns
the white silence of dacha snow,
imagines ice dendrites melting
on his tongue, his father's smile,
an heirloom glass, a silent toast
infused with ghosts & buffalo grass.

mechtatel (мечтатель) — dreamer

ПС

TsUM

Approaching TsUM as buskers chorus
everywhere that poets go
(their cornet sings) a dog's before us,
or two, for (does the doorman know
this tune?) these pug-like flat pilasters
were first conceived by Scottish masters:
he lets in lapdogs, slebs and sleaze
to a realm of Muir and Merrilies –
and both these names are deeply doggy,
so that's what Chekhov called his strays...
(best keep these mongrel bards at bay).
Now TsUM and GUM are more for moggies,
a must for brassy mugs, they bin
my childhood dream of Soviet tins.

BHX

Notes from the Undermind 3

Since Dundee stood as Moscow's double
for TV dramas' cheaper skates
I felt I'd fit with little trouble,
join that long queue of Scottish fakes
as MacMock-Muscovite, insider,
malcontent, phantom carriage-rider,
who moans as though from Petersburg.
And, since each urge must have its erg
I'd list each fixture, nose each neighbour,
and, like a deil amang them, sly
as sleepers, I'd be verse's spy.
Or so I thought, for all my labour
was like the scratchings of a ghost
now that my moleskine's notes are lost.

As though it were the world's ambition,
everything gets lost in time
while we are caught in intermission
still staying curtain fall with rhyme.
The facts, ma'am? We are sham or skiving –
no call, no script will be arriving,
no story but this one we pen,
we lost-beneath-attention men.
What are we like? Well, first, we're poets,
that cross-breed of the lark and skate
you barely have to read to hate;
and next we're Northern – we say 'bo-at'
and mean the ones our fathers built,
we're chippy, bolshy, filled with guilt.

Provincials, throwbacks, monolinguous –
though Andy's Russki's looking up –
Beneath the Underdog with Mingus?
More pissy like the underpup
(that book's a favourite of Mike Marra's –
Dundee's wee speug to Tom Wait's sparra).
We choose to roam the underground
and mark the limbless, drunk, unsound;
hear foundless fables while foundations
of Kremlin and Cathedral shake
like snow-caked wolves, as though they wake
and growl at their old pack of nations,
raise cyber-claws, bare gas-pipe fangs,
demand they all rejoin the gang.

BHX

Izmaylovo Park

Young Peter's model troop manoeuvres
still influence Izmaylovo Park:
the dogs all lie one way like hoovers
of morning heat, and dream of barks –
those sailors', airmens', soldiers' noses,
tankmen of Taganskaya's poses,
all point heroically the same
maiolica way, for such is fame
(or death). Here, silver girlish birches
sway like the drinkers of street beer,
breakfast of businessmen and bears!
And at the Metro's thermal churches
sobachki curl, curs in the sun –
Dame Metro warms all cursive bums.

sobachka (собачка) — doggie or pup; also the @ sign

BHX

sparrows & lovers

easter sun stoops;
makes silver-gilt of birch,
& charcoal shadows
dragged through ragged grass.
they tangle like the arms
of scrapping girls.

an old man carries a sapling,
hands cradling its frail limbs.
this moment contented
in its own sparse company.
stray dogs & ferris wheels,
fat sparrows & quiet lovers.

a host of gentle songs
launched into the blue.

ПС

Mayakovskaya I

We're staring at the sky's mosaic
Three hundred feet below the ground,
Where poetry becomes prosaic
And heaven is the wrong way round.
This monument to Soviet flyers
Conspires with our earth-bound desires
To soar above the rush-hour crowds
And join the stars behind the clouds.
Like Tantalus' fruits, they shimmer
Above our heads, each juicy peach
Within our grasp but out of reach.
The future fades, the stars grow dimmer.
But when the carriage doors slide to,
The sky beyond is just as blue.

ЭК

Mayakovskaya II

Mayakovskaya's 'Hours' see Frolov
roofing all Russia with one day:
its roundels' underground sky's roll of
foreshortened parachutists, stray
sunflowers, signalmen and vaulters –
leapers, goalkeepers, air's assaulters,
are lost in blue like songless larks –
their day preferring dawn to dark.
One drunken night Alexey Dushkin
showed us his grandfather's game in his hall:
sending a coin to orbit and fall
round steel-grooved arches – this much push can
flip time, till I look down, mid-trick:
the first coin in the five kopeck flick.

BHX

someone else's heaven

the smart-arse pubescent
in a bootleg *slipknot* hoodie
& cossack hat shouts
lazy obscenities at a pair
of pretty girls. they shrink
in unison like startled snails
into the quilted nylon shells
of almost matching anoraks.

there are zeppelins over mordor
dull skies succumbing to blue.
2 lads chase balsa gliders
with their eyes, cricking
their necks for a glimpse
of someone else's heaven.

ПС

Borovitskaya

He slides across the polished marble
On bubble-wrap instead of legs
He lost in Grozny or in Kabul.
She prays in Russian, though she begs
In perfect English. Life's persistent,
Though pain and loss are never distant.
A medieval tree motif
Picks out in rose-pink brick-relief
The fruits of fifteen Soviet nations
Still hanging in the brick-built tree
For every Moscow child to see,
Like ghosts of painful amputations,
All fallen, picked or left to rot
In someone else's private plot.

ЭК

Belichiy Gory

Bronze panels show in Belichiy Gory
the war between the Greys and Reds –
Yeltsin's high station tells the story
that left ten million squirrels dead.
One side were celto-Scythian rebels,
the other alien, sleepless devils:
Prince Nutkin, Tuftsky, Sasha Cheeks,
Tsar Timfy Tiptoes – through these peaks
from birch-top fought to floor of forest
while Greys made famine from Red's glut
for every tree, each twig, each nut.
Why was this iconised by Boris?
While oligarchic fat cats feast,
democracy is for the beasts.

BHX

Taganskaya

The walls of black and white ceramic
Are lined with copper bas-reliefs,
A post-Gagarin cool dynamic
Of Sixties space-race/age motifs.
These days such dreams of moonlit travel
Have lost their shine. The myths unravel
Like melting wings, the stars grow faint,
And earth's first blueness now seems quaint.
This future is already dated,
A memory of the human race
Before the Fall. We're lost in space
Within the maze ourselves created.
Our train arrives. Time we were gone.
And so the world sails calmly on.

ЭК

eucharist

the old couple adjacent have us engrossed
he places *moiva* on her tongue, as if the host,
undaunted by an acrid trace of desiccated piss
each sacrament's anointed with a salty kiss,
& each sets free their ancient lips to reminisce.

tonight we'll give the georgian lamb a miss
& find instead, on page 13, the perfect dish:
a paschal feast, 'a brotherhood of fish'
of gilded carp, of perch & infant pike
impaled upon a blackened spike.

their eyes are fixed on heaven still
though cataracted by the grill
& in their gaping, muted jaws
a frozen accusation thaws.

moiva (мойва) — dried and salted capelin.

ПС

Notes from the Undermind 4

Just as it took a team of Morlocks
to haul off Wells's time machine,
so reams of Persons bred in Porlock
cauterised Coleridge, healed his dreams.
(When wrecking boors draw all opprobrium
no need to mention pints of opium.)
How did the temporal traveller cope
on losing both device and hope?
Without a notebook I must gather
the scents of presence like a dog,
and treat my losses like a drug.
Just one year older than my father,
the Metro pulses like a man,
eludes me like that blank old Khan.

What did I lose? The scent of detail,
not stations, but their inbetweens –
that close, dull scarlet marble's foetal
passage, hot crowd-rush, someone seen,
half-noted – foetid breath of drinker,
some Dostoevskian student slinker –
that couple, he immense, she short,
their giggling, middle-aged rapport;
that bunch of full moon-peaked cap coppers
by a tunnel's fork – alert for thieves
or waiting for their shift's relief?
Some line on that mosaic newspaper
at Kievskaya; a tractor corp
who look like they want nothing more.

BHX

Tsaritsino

The Empress Park. A Gothic folly
Half-built by Catherine the Great;
A monument to tasteless lolly
That's richly placed to demonstrate
New money's love of tax-free charity.
Dressed-up as brash cash-flash vulgarity.
The self-made rich maintain the law
With hand-outs for the man-made poor,
Like something out of *Nasha Rasha* –
A Love Ball for St Valentine
(Official partner: Calvin Klein)
In aid of homeless children. Sasha
Points out the ruins round the lake;
But which are man-made, which are fake?

ЭК

Chkalovskaya

Change at Ice Station Chkalovskaya,
half whale's gut, half bright fuselage,
steel-ribbed for a Polar hero-flier
who left no print on the Arctic page,
but like Gargarin flew one mission
too far – fit subject for revision
if you plant flags where none can tread:
upon the North Pole's rich sea-bed.
So Putin echoes Soviet hubris
pasticheing power as design
(and chasing oil where ice declines);
he's warming up the Gulags' rubric –
this gullet says: the sky's a hole,
let every owl feast on moles.

BHX

Rimskaya

The harlot she-wolf feels the tugging
Of infant empires at her chest,
The milk-gorged young Madonna's hugging
The baby at her naked breast –
Medallions for all the mothers
Whose sons are murdered by their brothers.
Third International or Third Rome,
These seven hills are now the home
To these two shoeless toddlers crawling
Like empire-builders on their knees,
Among the ruins like refugees.
Their capitol's already falling.
The clashing symbols celebrate
Its status as a Third World state.

ЭК

mass

we're drawn like moths, in trance, towards
the spastic dance of votive flames, the opiate
lure of hope, of saccharin, frankincense &
myrrh. the silver island's onion domes seem
near; but dark is dark, & what we fear is not

a fabulist's bear or troll but skinheads pissed
on ethanol, whose bellies burn with want &
hate. the boys who bunked off school to fish
& smoke & whittle sap-soft spears & were
not taught the lexicon of 'wish' or even how

to punctuate the breathless lines of fate. the
sharp-cheeked boys with blooded, egg-yolk
eyes, whose golden carp remains, confined,
within the slick of this black pond, un-caught.

silver island (остров серебряный) — a man-made island on the
old Izmaylovo Estate (Усадьба Измайлово), home to the
Pokhorovoskiy Cathedral.

ПС

Relic

Tonight we follow our researches
(You see we don't do things by halves)
To one of Moscow's toy-town churches.
Inside old women wrapped in scarves
Stand clutching candles while the clergy
Perform their Easter thaumaturgy
In fuck-off beards and fuck-off hats
With some old dodgy relic that's
Being carried round upon a cushion
Accompanied by the pleasant drone
Of hierocratic baritone.
It lasts all night. How very Russian.
We head for Izmaylovsky Park
And leave them singing in the dark.

ЭК

29

Iconostasis

Just as a novel's not its foreword,
there are two types of time machine:
the kind that moves you back and forward,
and that which halts and holds the dream
pandemic of millennial motion,
its substitute a stunned devotion –
iconostasis, folding out
the present's tumbling cube of doubt
into a plane we face this Paskha
inside old Orthodoxy's church
where Lenin's masses, left mid-lurch,
await their Christ, their souls' task-master,
to finish harrowing His hell
and, tunnelling up, rake theirs as well.

BHX

Paskha

This Christ o' the neist thoosand years
(Hugh MacDiarmid)

Iconostasis keeps us out
by showing what's beyond all doubt
or what we put there, crowding up
to midnight in a Moscow suburb
heads scarfed, hands candled, icons kissed,
this wall is like a whelk's shut lid.
       Hristos voskres!
Behind it time's unlocked, Christ swims
like any sunk Aeneas – just
another Orphic drop-in, tourist
in Hell, a traveller through time's
five books, the Torah as the ages,
the unsaved dead trapped in its pages.
      Voistinu voskres!

Behind there's Tartarus for tsars
and party bosses too, Christ rolls
along his ghost rail past them all –
Ivan a pan-fried fricassee
and Peter face down in the swamp,
Dis's foundations on his rump.
      Hristos voskres!
Lenin must hammer at an anvil
with bared brows, forging manacles
for his own wrists, while Stalin's trimmed
moustache-made-sickle slices him
in ever finer crimson sheets –
and Marx and Engels are redeemed.
      Voistinu voskres!

A moment's darkness stands for all
that death, as every million martyrs
just need a few good murderers:
one light, and then the icons walk
off the wall, shouldered by the surge
of people orbiting the church
      Hristos voskres!
Time bulges in a droplet from
light's little door, the conquered tomb;
raw time, without direction, meets
their singing lips, the crowd, the priests,
their hymn inseminates the hour
while death and reason seem to cower.
      Voistinu voskres!

That morning, leaving the hotel,
we'd heard a choir practising
their scales, just in the carpark, singing
as Orpheus once tuned up Hell
as though the spheres and socialism
had never felt the breath of schism.
      Hristos voskres!
Now, standing in the emptied nave,
we watch babushkiy start to brush;
the screen feels blanker than the grave
while underneath us comes a rush:
one coach, beneath the underground,
in which a head goes round and round.
      Voistinu voskres!

Hristos voskres. Voistinu voskres (Христос воскрес. Войстину воскрес) — 'Christ is risen.' 'Indeed he is risen' (traditional exchange at Paskha, the Orthodox Easter)

BHX

Novodevichiy

The cemetery gates are closing
and, for today, we're locked outside;
while Moscow's names, Medusa-chosen,
stare back above, their bones all ride
Death's *Metro-Tri*, just six feet under,
whose route is rot, whose tracks' low thunder
has not yet reached a living ear –
the worm's a subtle engineer.
They circulate beneath our notice,
the coffins of the litterateurs,
les poetes allongés, les fleurs
du Malchik; playwrights lose the plot as
composers decompose, dead tales
are scratched on lids with fingernails.

BHX

The Worst Concoctions, vol. 1

'For reasons the justification of which it is not for me to attempt, the Russian public... commenced some years ago to take an interest in my work. Free of the literary temperament is supposed to be of vanity, I confess to some feelings of pride in the honour thus accorded to me. Of late, my gratification has been considerably marred, however, by my powerlessness to prevent the issue of unauthorized translations, which, so I am assured by my Russian friends, are at the best garbled and incorrect and at the worst concoctions...'

Jerome K. Jerome, letter to *The Times*, July 8 1902

Against the Current

from a lost play (unlikely to be by Vladimir Mayakovsky)

A river scene. Bird song. Weeping willows trail in the water. Shooting stars. It is snowing. An ice-breaker. On deck are THREE MEN *and* A DOG.

FIRST MAN	Brrrr. It's jolly cold.
SECOND MAN	I say, are we there yet?
FIRST MAN	Where?
SECOND MAN	There.
FIRST MAN	Where?
SECOND MAN	Where we are going.
FIRST MAN	Where are we going?
SECOND MAN	Blowed if I can remember.
THIRD MAN	I think we're there.
FIRST MAN	Where?
THIRD MAN	Here.
SECOND MAN	What do you mean, we are here?
THIRD MAN	I mean we're here.
FIRST MAN	How do you know?
THIRD MAN	Well I'm certainly here.
SECOND MAN	Ah – but can you be sure?
THIRD MAN	Look, it says on this map – 'You Are Here'.
SECOND MAN	Ah - but where, exactly, is Here?
THIRD MAN	What do you mean, 'where is Here'? Here is here.
FIRST MAN	But how do we know it is not over there?
THIRD MAN	Because in that case the map would say 'You Are Over There'. But it doesn't. It plainly says, 'You Are Here'.
FIRST MAN	Well I wish I wasn't. Here I mean. I wish I was somewhere else.

THIRD MAN	Where?
FIRST MAN	A nice warm pub. Roaring fire. A plate of beefsteak and porter. Hot muffins.

Enter a Pirate ship. ADMIRAL KOLCHAK *is at the wheel, dressed as Long John Silver. Behind him are* GENERAL WRANGEL, WOODROW WILSON, LLOYD GEORGE, GEORGES CLEMENCEAU *and* BENITO MUSSOLINI *on monocycles.*

PIRATE CAPTAIN	Did someone say hot muffins? All aboard!

THE PIRATES *jump onto the icebreaker.* THE FIRST MAN *hits* LLOYD GEORGE *on the head with a banjo.* THE SECOND MAN *throws a tin of pineapple.* THE DOG *barks. After a brief struggle the victorious* PIRATES *raise the Jolly Roger.*

PIRATE CAPTAIN	Seize them! Put the prisoners in chains!
FIRST MAN	Why?
SECOND MAN	Don't argue.
THIRD MAN	What do we have to lose?

THE PRISONERS *are put in chains.*

PIRATE CAPTAIN	Where are the muffins?
FIRST MAN	Muffins?
SECOND MAN	What muffins?
THIRD MAN	We don't have any muffins.
PIRATE CAPTAIN	Very well. Let them walk the plank!

THE PRISONERS *are led towards the plank.* MUSSOLINI *plays the Dead March from Saul on the banjo.*

FIRST MAN   Look out! We're heading straight
                       towards the rapids!
THE PRISONERS   Help! Help! Somebody help!

They jangle their chains as the boat spins towards the edge of the waterfall.

SECOND MAN   I say, who is that chap over there?

THE MAN FROM THE FUTURE *walks across the water. He has holes in his hands and his head is on fire.*

THE MAN FROM
THE FUTURE   Greetings Comrades.
                       History is a torrent
                       That has burst its sides.
                       On the furthest banks
                       They are building
                       The cities of tomorrow
                       With the energy of the stars,
                       The smiles of tigers
                       And the smell of hot muffins.

He parts the waves. THE PRISONERS *escape to the safety of the river bank. The sound of cheering and motor-horns.* THE PIRATES *are swept over the edge of the rapids. More cheers.*

THE MAN FROM
THE FUTURE   What do you think of the show so far?
THE DOG   Ruff!

CURTAIN

ЭК

37

Idle was My Springtime

Sergei Esenin did not write this

Idle was my springtime,
Days of youth and ease,
Drifting on the river
Through the sleepy trees.

Merry were my comrades,
Still the afternoon,
Nights we drank together
Neath the wide-eyed moon.

Violent was October,
Bringing bayonet snows;
In the iron morning
The water meadows froze.

Farewell childhood memories,
Adieu my village friends,
The swallow leaves his nest
When the summer ends.

My craft is now the Song
I sing for Mother Russia,
And when I run aground
Lenin helps to push her.

ЭК

Crush the Parasites!

from a 1935 poster, words probably not by Demyan Bedny

The Saboteur's stuffing his mattress with roubles,
The Kulak is hiding his gold in the straw,
The Trotskyite creeps like a wolf in the forest,
The émigré generals are dreaming of war.

On Guard! On Guard!
Throw the bourgeois in the river
And make the bastards shiver!

But in England the bourgeois their banjos are strumming,
The ship of state lazily drifts down the stream,
Unaware of the storm that is certainly coming
They sit drinking sweet milky tea with the queen.

On Guard! On Guard!
Throw the bourgeois in the flames,
Throw the idlers in the Thames!

Now the workers are marching on Buckingham Palace
Where Robin Hood chopped off the head of King John
To smash every Orthodox icon and chalice
And chase Mr Churchill away till he's gone.

On Guard! On Guard!
Grab the bourgeois by the trouser!
Throw the porkers in the Yauza!

ЭК

Ophelia

from an unfinished sequence not by Anna Akhmatova

She is a dancer
In the river's mirror.
Lamps gutter
Under the trees.
Three men.

Three graves.
In the darkness
A banjo sings.
O hunger!
O pineapples…

ЭК

Nocturne

not from Boris Pasternak's diary

Rain drips through the trees,
Oars beat time in the water,
Only the rain knows
The fathomless songs of the river.

The swans beat their wings like pages
In a book we cannot follow,
A dog lies still in the rushes
Under a weeping willow.

On the distant shore of Galilee
The charcoal evening dies,
And the mosquito stars shine
Like two lovely black eyes.

ЭК

41

Like Corsairs

author unknown, except that it's not Yevgeny Yevtushenko

When the thaw came
                    we were looking the other way.
It took us a long time
                    before we heard
the cracks splitting the ice
                    on the Oka river
like new lines
          on an old map.
It took us a long time
                    before we could hear
the birds reading their poems
                        in the forests,
solemn as children
              in the Hall of Columns,
the icicles melting away
                  like critics
and the roar of the river
                    adding its applause
to the standing ovation
              of Spring.
We found the old boat
                where we moored it in Summer.
With two friends
            and my old hunting dog
We pushed out
          into the crazy waters
Newly liberated
          from Winter's regime.

The name of our Brigantine
                        was *Freedom*.
Like corsairs,
            we took no prisoners,
only what a poet needs –
                        cigarettes, a pen,
the music of the wind
                    and the wide flowing river of humanity.
We followed the stars
                    until we came to an island.
The monkeys welcomed us
                    like old friends.
At night we eat tinned fruit
                    and stuffed trout,
And light tall fires
                on the white sands,
Waiting for the rest of the world
                            to join us.

ЭК

Notes from the Undermind 5

I often dream about the Tower:
its sixties brain-dead concrete bulk
half-steampunk city, half-prog bower;
its shabby lifts that blink and sulk;
its ground floor's empty-shelved emporia
sleep's metaphor for my aporia;
its bored first floor a restaurant
that either won't revolve, or can't
stop speeding up till dizzied diners
spew, while its stew of dense-packed flats
ascends in fumes of boots and cats –
my block, detached the way a liner
or a starship is, a haunt of Welles
that wakes up here as our hotel.

Its complex pairs off drab skyscrapers:
six back to back room-duellists –
their layout gave poor Andy vapours,
he'd right turn leftly in a mist;
not pissed, but merely mirror-minded,
descend a staircase as he climbed it.
While Paul and I would break our fast
he'd wander like the Dutchman's mast.
Pelmeni, blini, buckwheat, herring,
and coffee from a stained steel tank –
we feasted, chatted, planned and drank;
meanwhile, past florists, banks, unerring
he trailed and failed to fill his tum –
replete, we'd meet him, chewing gum.

For me, the child of Scottish multis
whose father joined the Party young,
the Metro flipped his communal cult as
life underground, but linked along
its buried halo hubbed with stations:
all towers inverted, all our nations
compressed, as though in outer space.
I dreamt of cafes, homes, by grace
of digging, safe as fallout shelters;
of galleries like ribs of light
encased with muscled earth for night;
each level reached by gentle skelter
as calm as libraries, not graves:
laboratories of the saved!

BHX

the taste of nothing

like cerberus tamed
a dog called saturday
licks the bleeding feet
of a dead-eyed mongol
whose soul has drowned
in the taste of nothing.
the pastel, nylon weave
of his laundry bag life
tumescent, like the cheeks
of a rank, bulimic hamster.

& here, where the air is moist
with the breath of our departures
we'll navigate a stoic bow
through sheol's frail legato hum

ПС

Komsomolskaya I

They sprawled like dogs before the pillars:
Komsomolskaya's pack of drunks,
confined to vodka's reptile cellars –
their brains' black hole where all hope's sunk.
The pavement trailed puke and saliva
from one old drunken Lord Godiva's
gob, naked in his shit-streaked suit,
where underground his state-spent youth
slaved so a mosaic of Twisty Jesus
could parallel stern Lenin's face
(at least since Stalin was replaced).
Time-travellers catch strange diseases
from others' futures, fevered pasts:
When so much sorrow's drowned, what lasts?

BHX

stigmata

this place not shrine but crypt;
for the ill-taught & ill-equipped.

a mournful claxon broke the news.
the sky, rain-charged, a dusty bruise;

so fathers choked & mothers wept,
while muted, sanguine tendrils crept

to colonise the fallen stones,
anoxic clay & splintered bones.

an honour bed for broken dreams,
an epitaph for unheard screams

& let the wishful bear the scars,
their fingers pricked on thorny stars.

the virgin blood of a *komsomol* martyr
lyophilized in rusted quartz stigmata.

komsomol (Комсомол) — Communist Union of Youth, many of
whom assisted the construction on the Moscow Metro.

ПС

Komsomolskaya II

The friezes trace the usual story
From Borodino to Berlin,
A narrative of martial glory
In which the heroes always win.
No doubt all empires have pretended
That sacrifice and death are splendid,
But when the world's one hope becomes
Reduced to rifles, flags and drums
The cause is lost. Outside the station
The ranks of sun-brown drunks play dead,
A pair of shoes by every head;
They're bedding down for the duration
In blood and piss, their wounds concealed,
Like heroes on a battlefield.

ЭК

Comrade Bear

Eh saw um sklent
                    fae thi side o meh eh
medved at Sviblovo,
                    a bear on an escalator, amid
thi coats of airms, the letters
in anodised Church Slavonic aluminium.

Thi bear descendin thru thi platform
gangin doon wi nae murmel o sang
tae thi hinny belly core
                    cucurbit o sweet lava
wi thi glow pollen globes tae licht his wey
tae whaur thi blin bees
                    glammach an stir,
lady Cossack insecks wi thir spears
turning thi deid
            owre and owre
                        i thi glaizie glaur.

Eh saw thi bear descend tae glowr
at pharaohs and tsars
preservit in glycerine and tar
Triassic in aspic
                Jurassic in amber
            borassic i thi braziers and mire.

medved (медведь) — a bear.

sklent — sideways; *murmel* — murmur; *hinny* — honey; *glammach* — snap at; *glaizie* — glittering, sleek; *glaur* — sticky mud; *borassic* — penniless.

BHX

Loco

We're greeted at the Metro station
By riot-police with snatch-squad vans,
A heavy-handed operation
Ignored by all the Loco fans.
Soon both ends of the ground are ringing
With shirtless polyphonic singing,
The international belly-dance
Of those who haven't got a chance.
A penalty might change the story
(Although he seemed a mile offside)
But then he puts the bastard wide.
The crowd erupts in silent fury.
The final score – what else? – nil-nil.
In Russian 'fan' means 'one who's ill'.

ЭК

Ode: re Spartak FC

Hail to Paul, Blyth Spartan,
footballer thou never wert –
not unlike Dumbarton,
well, perhaps more alert –
but could thee/should thee/would thee wear an Irn-Bru shirt?

Run that OMON's gauntlet,
truncheon jerk and horse,
Loko fans, undaunted,
strolled between brute force
and swollen rumours of disorder (lies, of course).

Play was enervating –
draughts instead of chess;
chorus syncopating
choriambic stress,
the ground a resonating Trans-Siberian express.

You became emotive
at incompetence
echoed Lokomotiv's
choochoo 'Loko' chants,
critiquing Spartak Nalchik's notional defence.

Poets should fill stadia –
so the great lie goes,
verse in that Arcadia
beating hollow prose:
its feet supplying Route One dogma to the proles.

Be that poet hidden
in a football crowd,
publish what's unwritten
though it's yelled out loud —
a task no harder, surely, than putting shorts on clouds.

Hail to Comrade Peanut:
football, you'll agree,
needs the link between it
and hegemony
revealed for all these blinded referees to see.

BHX

Song of the Loco Fans

We don't need vodka, we don't need gin,
All we want is a Lokomotiv win.
(Football supporters song)

Revolutions are the locomotives of History
(Nikita Krushchev)

Everybody's doing a brand new dance now
(Come on comrade, do the Locomotiv)
Everybody's saying we don't stand a chance now
(Come on comrade, do the Locomotiv)
But we travel round the country watching Loco play
Its easier than learning your *ABV*,
So come on, come on,
Do the Locomotiv with us.

Watching Locomotiv drives us round the bend now
(Come on comrade, do the Locomotiv)
We don't know how to shoot and we just can't defend now
(Come on comrade, do the Locomotiv)
But thanks to Russian Railways we're back on track,
And under Rashid Rakhimov* we won't look back,
So come on, come on,
Do the Locomotiv with us.

Although we're not as wealthy as Abramovitch now
(Come on comrade, do the Locomotiv)
As long as Bilyaletdinov** is on the pitch now
(Come on comrade, do the Locomotiv)
We're gonna win the league like in 2004,
We're gonna play in Europe like we did before,
So come on, come on,
Do the Locomotiv with us.

You gotta swing your hips now
Come on, come on,
Do the Locomotiv with us,
Yeah
You gotta eat those chips now
Come on, come on,
Do the Locomotiv,
Do the Lokomotiv,
Do the Lokomotiv with us.

*He's gone!
**Already sold!

ЭК

polonaise

define me today
by what i am not

not by the recalled
but things forgotten

a destiny still plastic
all our histories spastic

a pretty busker plays
oginski's *polonaise*

an avalanche slump
of maudlin notes

descending the curves
of her early pregnancy

held breath in the strings
in the soft knots of matrix.

ПС

Base

To Kitai-Gorod and to OGI,
A bargain-basement bookshop bar
That serves cold fish and hot *pirogi*
Beneath the earth, a Shangri-la
Of dark and smoky book-lined cellars.
We eat while Sonya tries to tell us
That though the city she calls home
Is many-hued, not monochrome,
There's still the Troglodyte persuasion,
Those animals afraid of light,
Who see the world in black and white
And think her features too *Caucasian*.
The smoke throws shadows on the walls
Like primitive graffiti scrawls.

ЭК

cabaret

i catch her smiling, eyes half-bowed,
as we discuss the hold of faith (too loud);
from byzantine iconoclasts to soviet kitsch,
the vodka's nudged our volume switch;
we're on a roll, we're in full swing,
it seems there's not a single thing
beyond the big-brained cabaret,
no bull-shit theory we can't convey

& she'll presume we're mad or pissed,
or both, which isn't that far from the truth,
not only that, she's spotted we're devoid
of youth. her smile's dissolved, the moment's
missed, another moscow beauty will go
un-kissed, by us at least. by us at least.

ПС

The Voice of the Morlock

'Tis the voice of the Morlock, I heard it exclaim
'Caucasians are negros – we know who to blame,
these menial Armenians we murder and maim,
these Khazaks and Tajiks, they're all just the same –
> *We're not what we were but a Morlock has bite:*
> *we shall dine on their flesh till the end of the night!*

'We're poor but we're *über*, our hate has a name:
they rape Russia's maidens, pour sluts on the game,
they blow up apartments – the FSB's tame:
Herr Hitler would halt them, our war was a shame –
> *Sure, Morlocks got killed, still, Nazis are right:*
> *by the digging of graves we shall reach for the heights!*

'Our glorious future, like vodka from grain,
must be distilled from all underdogs' pain,
so down to the Metro and let's board a train:
we'll stamp on these fleas till we're Russians again –
> *We're not what we will be but Morlocks have might:*
> *wash your eyes in their blood until you've seen the light!'*

BHX

lolita

the train arrives; a band-saw
blade through awkward knots.
it drags a wake of banya heat
infused with musk & engine oil.

shark-eyed & sharp-tongued,
lolita basks in the glare of her
confidence, her sculpted hair
as fragile as her golden youth.

she's got that skin that sheens
like lathe-cut clay. as pure as
safely-sourced Class As or those
minimalist frangipani bouquets.

the lazy swoop of her sponsor's name is
tattooed on the arc of her shallow breast.

ПС

VDNKh

Here fans of *Sovok* memorabilia
Who need to scratch nostalgia's itch
Could overdose on the familiar
Lysenko girl-meets-tractor kitsch
Displayed in faux-folk art pavilions
As tribute from the Empire's millions.
Where Stalin stood, now someone's job
Is dressing-up as *Goobka Bob* –
A perfect emblem for the Nashists
Who gather here to say their prayers,
Who think the past is only theirs
And who like all good neo-Fascists
Dislike the future just because
It isn't what it never was.

Sovok (Совок) — a sarcastic term for the Soviet Union; *Goobka Bob* (Губка Боб) — SpongeBob Squarepants.

ЭК

Stalker

Which was the Writer, who was Stalker?
True, no Professor knows his way,
but who'll find the banya but this talker
to shoppers? Or VDNKh,
that Zone where SpongeBob posed with Lenin?
(Bizarre pavilions, gross as Blenheim,
where gold and wheat and maidens blend
in lies of plenty Hell can't mend.)
I confess my haircut quest, 'Go *Streeshka*!'
did stretch the patience of a Paul...
um... *pareekhmahyerskay'* you all?
But let's let trios off the leash-ka:
no Harris or George or J's remarks;
no Harpo, Chico or Grouch – just Marx.

streeshka (стрижка) — haircut; *pareekhmahyerskaya*
(парикмахерская) — barbershop.

BHX

To Say Nothing of the Dog

Let's hear it for the race of giants
Who named this station in the hope
That Nature could be tamed by science;
The world seen through a microscope
Reveals the secrets of the ages
As simple as a text book's pages.
But every sonnet has a but
And this butt has a tail – a mutt.
Now science has fallen out of fashion
They've built a statue here in praise
Of underdogs and homeless strays,
A big-eyed symbol of Compassion
And dog-eared Disney-kitsch. Behold –
Its polished nose has turned to gold.

ЭК

Mendeleevskaya

Mendeleevskaya, home to Malchik
(although we didn't know that then)
began this futurist-nostalgic
project: it made us Metromen.
Its light were spindled, mock-atomic,
its platform spacious, yet entomic:
it was a scifi paradigm
that shrank-and-sent you back through time.
And here it was the supermodel
sank a stiletto in the eye
of Malchik, leaving him to die –
a stray who'd been *malako*-coddled
by all babushkiy, here his bones
are sanctified, a cur in bronze.

This scabby dog's tale may sound fancy
concocted by the desperate
whose poem lacks a Montmorency
yet have to make their symbols fit.
But no, far from it, wait, *prasteetyeh*,
the truth is always that bit neater:
there was a Malchik, beaten up
(by someone rich or by a cop)
commemorated by a statue
that signifies New Russia's woes,
and so above gets thrown below:
just as the Metro's a buried '*hachoo*,'
Malchik's its Laika, Stalin's its tsar,
and hope is a kennel, boiled in the stars.

malako (молоко) — milk; *prasteetyeh* (простите) — excuse me;
hachoo (я хочу) — I want

BHX

64

Metaphor for Malchik

Dogs don't use metaphor
(Ruth Padel)

I have been burying the delicious white stick.
I have been sniffing the butthole's brown flower.
I have caught the wooden wingbone:
here it is.

I have returned to the stomach's liquid child,
to the lumpy feast. I have been licking
my own soft chestnuts:
here they are.

Why do you tug the neck's strap-on tail
when this Volga of hot bitch-scent
has just poured past?
There she is.

I make a tripod fountain.
I puddle up to the gadget of my new ipoodle.
I cock a wood'll woo her:
here it is.

She is squatting mother to the fragrant slug.
I am not distracted by the magnetic North
South East and West Poles of wee wee:
but there they are.

She's like the leg of a Chekhovian aunt
I must embrace. She's like the trousers
of the garden invader, ripe for perforation.
So she is.

She's like the white hole in the black air
that sucks out howls. She's like the tendons
that tug the skeleton of the pack together. In fact,
here we are.

BHX

Smelly

For once the poet Herbert's mapless
And we're stuck up some dusty street,
Three men in Moscow, hot and hapless.
Napoleon's army in retreat
Cannot have felt so tired and weary.
We're contemplating hara-kiri.
The *banya* which should be round here
Has disappeared. That much is clear.
It doesn't matter. Herbert's driven
By voices which insist we find
The perfect *banya* of the mind,
Where all our doubts shall be forgiven –
Brave paradise of steam and soap!
He thinks we're almost there. Some hope.

smeliy (смелый) — bold, brave

ЭК

Astrakhanskiy

To find, I claimed, a local *banya*
from Prospekt Mira can't be hard,
but that's ignoring the *otstraniye*
of dragging two reluctant bards.
The place's name was Astrakhanskiy –
a chance to lose your fur and prance-ski,
skeletal in its cleansing heat –
if we could just locate the street.
First Andy asked two Moscow maidens
and then he asked a bored young cop:
none of them knew, so his questions stopped.
'Gdye banya?' I enquired, unbidden,
of *piva*-booths, though (this made me shy)
I couldn't follow their reply.

Some bloke with perfect beer-flecked English
sent us right back the miles we'd trudged
and it grew harder to distinguish
my dear friends' grins from grim-faced grudge
as in a maze of new *pereuloks*
we mithered like three blinded morlocks
until a shopper's headscarfed nod:
unsmiling, silently, she showed
us to that sanctuary, the *banya*,
where heat defeats the hand you're dealt
and even Andy's frown must melt,
where in the loft's infernal *stantsia*
we met old men in pixie hats
with genitals like dangling bats.

otstraniye (отстрание) — estrangement; *gdye* (где) — where
(pronounced as a monosyllable); *piva* (пиво) — beer; *pereulok*
(переулок) — lane

BHX

A Welcome to the *Banya*

The Mobster and the Businessman
    climbed to the hottest steps
and sprawled there for the longest time
    for they were heat's adept –
while others sweated, wept or plunged
    they spread their towels and slept.

And dreamt they were transformed into
    a Lobster and a Clam
who steamed upon a barbecue
    as innocent as lamb
till, crimson-clawed and open-shelled,
    they sang like old Khayyam.

They sang, 'Because we're nearly cooked
    the truth can now be told:
Hell's nothing but a *banya* where,
    because the world is cold,
we curl up to a devil and
    forget that God's a scold.'

'What are we like?' the Lobster cried,
    the Clam, amused, declared,
'We're mad as a bat on a tractor,
    and helpful as a bear;
and on the Metro, grateful pigs,
    we travel free as hares.'

They sang, 'There is a second sun
    as black as bile and ink
that freezes up this wicked world
    and rises as ours sinks,
and through the night its anti-light
    censors us – or so we think.'

'What do we know?' the Clam enquired,
    the Lobster laughed and said,
'You know that money is a lie
    and capital is dead;
I know where all the bodies try
    to find their loose-lipped heads.'

They suddenly awoke, and glared
    about them in the heat,
in case a so-called *droog* had heard
    what they sang in their sleep,
saw nothing but some Brits, so shared
    a final verse or three…

'No Heaven for the holy, right?
    No Limbo for the numb,
we know where you are going so
    we don't care where you're from:
the Metro always brings you here:
    log in at hell.com.'

droog (друг) — pal

BHX

Song of the *Banya*

Not enough bathhouses, not enough soap.
(Vladimir Mayakovsky)

In this city of well-dressed ambition
   It is hard to peel off from the dance,
But here in the *banya*, we say *do svidanya*
To all of that hustle and hassle and bustle –
   For once in the *banya*,
You've nothing to lose but your pants. Hey!

Hit me with your venik stick,
Hit me! Hit me!

As long as you're stark bollock naked
   You can stay in the *banya* all day,
The fat and the skinny, the max and the mini,
The lean and the gristly, the clean and the bristly,
   We sit in the *banya*
And sweat all our troubles away. Hey!

Hit me with your venik stick,
Hit me! Hit me!

The *banya* asks nobody questions,
   The *banya* tells nobody lies,
You jump in the water, your manhood gets shorter,
You walk in a mobster and crawl out a lobster,
   The god of the *banya*
Cuts every man right down to size. Hey!

Hit me with your venik stick,
Hit me! Hit me!

There's only one rule in the *banya*,
   Enlightened self-interest's our cause,
You may be quite podgy, you may look right dodgy
Be sick and unhealthy, or virile and wealthy,
   But here in the *banya* –
If you scrub my back, I'll scrub yours. Hey!

Hit me with your venik stick,
Hit me! Hit me!

The *banya* treats all men as brothers,
   The wise man, the fool and the knave,
No matter how ruthful or truthful you may be,
No matter how youthful you were as a baby,
   Outside of the *banya*
The next place we're equal's the grave. Hey!

Hit me with your venik stick,
Hit me! Hit me!

One member one soap is our slogan,
   Uniting the whole human race,
Once step through the door you can't tell the dirt poor
From the man with the itch to become stinking rich –
   If the world was a *banya*
It wouldn't be such a foul place. Hey!

Hit me with your venik stick,
Hit me! Hit me!

do svidanya (до свидания) — goodbye; *venik* (веник) — a bundle
of twigs (usually birch or oak) with which visitors to the *banya* hit
each other in order to increase blood circulation

ЭК

The Secret Moon

The dogs were pissing openly as if in a dream
(Soleiman Adel Guémar)

Our scarlet friend began to croon,
'There is a second, secret moon
that sank from space through Baikal's floor
and circles round our molten core,
that little sun that cannot glow.
When it, eclipsing, sits below
old Mother Moscow, all our drunks,
our *eezgoi*, trouser-spraying skunks,
each *beech*, each *bomzh, alcash or pyan,*
bradyagi wandering where they can,
is turned into a well-kicked dog
who, fleching, at a three-leg jog
takes muzzle to the nearest drain
and howls at every Metro train.
Then jumps the barriers, gammy pup –
the escalator may go up,
still he runs down it, joins the crowd
of platform peers, the Great Unproud,
they sniff each keester, piss and whine,
then fling themselves upon the line
before each metro's rush and grind,
since under-moonlight fills each mind
and they mistake the shuddered rail
for that below-globe's mining trail.

Sometimes an eager hound sticks out
his head in time to take a clout
that swipes it off, still in its hat –
the pack all chase it like a rat.
I've seen one bounce and blink in shock
as if it rolled through liquid rock
just like their moon beneath our feet,
still dust-free, craterless, complete.
And that is why I sit and sweat,
since even drunk I can't forget.'

eezgoi, beech, bomzh, alcash, pyan (изгой, бич, бомж, алкаш, пьян)
— a collection of terms for the temporarily or more
permanently drunk and homeless; *bradyagi* (бродяги) —
wanderers.

BHX

Orpheus on the Underground

The lower depths. October. Morning.
As we ascend towards the day
The poet Herbert, without warning
Decides to go the other way –
His shoe's caught in the escalator
That's taking him to his creator;
We wave goodbye, he says his prayers,
Then someone stops the moving stairs.
A close shave with a happy ending –
Instead of being swallowed whole
The poet's merely lost his sole –
A joke which he's no doubt intending
To celebrate in Orphic song.
Next time, perhaps, he'll lose his tongue.

ЭК

Oktyabrskaya

Ascending to the arch of trumpets –
Oktyabrskaya's brassy trill –
I left its crypt, that pseudo-sun-pit,
our future blue 'behind the grille' –
until the escalator's summit,
where, like a Wallace lacking Grommit,
my trainer's heel got nipped, then ripped,
near-swallowed by the stair-rod's grip;
the *dezhurnaya*, whose sole duty's
to sit there like a watchful slug
and hit the panic button, shrugs –
I'm staircase-*dejeuner*, my foot is –
whoa! – it's following my shoe:
this metal boa's learnt to chew!

A *Militsiya*, touched by pity,
halts the machinery just in time:
one sole aflap I hail the city
by walking like a tar-foot mime.
Some *sooper*glue and it's soon mended –
my wits, though, well-chewed, have descended
to where my rubber tongue would go,
slid through Polyakov's grille below
to where Our Lady of the Snakebite
must lick at Stalin's poisoned boot,
Eurydice, coiled round his loot;
his underground of brass and bakelite,
of pleather thrones and dialless phones,
where all the tracks are human bones.

dezhurnaya (дежурная) — escalator attendant

BHX

the holy lance

beneath the gilt-less stucco
of another slab of martial art
a legless veteran cuts a patient,
stuttering arc, through other
people's intact limbs. his chariot,
a piano cart, emblazoned with
a sacred heart, our lady
of kazan. one fist propels,
the other steers. longinus,
captain, keeper of the spears.

the non-negotiable terms of fate,
condemned to this, beyond escape;
two spastic stumps made conjugate
with bubble-wrap & gaffer tape.

ΠC

Sportivnaya

Good Comrade Mole, you're earth's curator,
its buried secrets' secret king,
its *Metro-dva* worm-script's translator;
archived within your burrowings
is where that Orphic head is shunted
so that the dead might be confronted
each grimy subterranean dawn
and let the Metro be reborn.
Or rather you're the small director
of these few empty upstairs rooms
in Sportivnaya – glass case tombs
for medals, maps, an old projector,
a TARDIS filled with mock-controls –
how slow the mole digs, now it's old.

'We had a plan – it's confidential –
had Germans breached the Metro...' 'Flood?'
I asked – too quick, not deferential.
He tried to catch the tell-tale nod
within his beard, and look as tricksy
as a loyal moleman can, sixty-
odd years late, Metro-loving geek
who could talk trains for several weeks
and would have... Quitting his museum,
(good cognac left as *spasiba*)
some camera'd clown went brassica:
took lawless snaps where cops could see him –
though saved from the cells by Sonya's plea,
'Eedyot! Angleeski!' – he's not. He's me.

Metro-dva (Метро-два) — Metro 2 (the secret secondary metro
system popularly believed to run beneath and alongside the
Metro); *spasiba* (спасибо) — thank you.

BHX

Three Men Build the Metro

In Eisenstein's lost 1938 film, 'Three Men Build the Metro' Comrade Podger leads other English students at the Lenin School in Moscow in singing this song. Words not by Yevgeny Dolmatovsky from The Worst Concoctions, vol.1.

Jolly digging weather,
The workers all agree
We will dig for ever,
Until all mankind is free,
Swing, swing together,
And onwards to victory,
Swing, swing together,
And onwards to victory.

Others will fill our places,
But we'll show them just what to do,
We'll put them through their paces,
Until they are diggers too,
And youth will be still in our faces,
When we cheer for the Metro crew,
And youth will be still in our faces,
When we cheer for the Metro crew.

The bourgeois may think they're clever,
And saboteurs make a row,
But we'll dig for ever
For the comrades we've left in Slough,
And nothing in life shall sever,
The chains that are round us now,
And nothing in life shall sever,
The chains that are round us now.

ЭК

Song of the Construction Worker

Remember when we couldn't read
and all our shoes were made of bark
we lived as though below in darkness
and everything was like a myth?
To each according to his need?
   It's possible it was, it's possible it was...

When Comrade Stalin set a task,
remember how our trust in him,
enthusiasm, youthful limbs
made myth seem like the truth?
Dig for the future, destroy the past —
   and it was possible, yes, it was possible...

BHX

germinal

beneath this arbat honour bed unmade
the broken skulls & vermeil braid
of   gouty *zemstvo* & cossack brave,
of inbred despot & jester knave,

chalky bones & usurped thrones
the overthrown & overblown
dissolving in a marshy broth
the essence of the behemoth.

& when they sank this frozen shaft
the miners & the soldiers laughed
carrion gorged on bourgeois words,
the corpses of imperial birds.

the laughter spread like heinous germs
it seeped, ten full wet fathoms below,
where comrade mole & comrade worm
sipped absinthe in gehinnom's glow

zemstvo (Земство) — pre-revolutionary local councils instituted
by Alexander II's quasi-liberal reforms.

ПС

Comrade Mouse

(after Elena Shvarts)

Doon here aa warlds are done
beginnin:
that yin abune wi a girn,
and this ablow
wi nae mane ava, a howe
that's wheesht and
dumb –

There's still the skeetir
o Comrade Meesh,
a moose
loose in thi dreamin machine.

Rair through faur-aff girders,
hool aaready nearbeh,
braith o rat
waarms yir fiss.
A moose rins alang thi Myetro rail –
but naw, it's aaready his ghaist.

abune — above; *girn* — groan, complaint; *ablow* — below; *mane* —
moan; *howe* — hollow; *wheesht* — silenced; *skeetir* — skitter; *rair*
— roar; *hool* — owl.

BHX

May Day

The sun is out. We're near the Duma.
It's International Workers' Day;
The crowds are swelling like the rumour
Of something better on the way.
Where Marx still struggles from the granite
To lead what once was half the planet,
The scarlet banners straggle past,
A grim procession at half-mast
That's one half proud, and one half-hearted,
Pursued by eager camera-crews
Who know poor turn-outs make good news.
Yabloko's rally should have started
In what was once Dzerzhinksy Square,
We march across. But no-one's there.

ЭК

four winds

four winds blow cold.
a haemorrhage of half-
formed moon will wrap
these scourging clouds
in crimson shrouds.

where lilya & maria had
swooned, the imprint of
an exit wound, a cordite
trace, an end to grace,
an archipelago of blood.

the sword is mightier than
the pen. denial so much
easier than truth. repeat
after me. repeat after we.

ПС

the long shadow

the grey square hisses
with the melody of vacuum.
a dilatory crowd ebbs
pursued & proceeded
by a legion of shadows.

& the grass is re-sown,
another winter endured
another dose of hope
procured from ashen
blokes at pavement bars.

all history is here, reflected
in the eyes of a pitiful dog.
christ is risen; indeed he is risen.
christ is risen. & with him the devil.

ПС

Pegasus' Stables

Yesenin drank here in the twenties,
Bulgakov used to live upstairs,
Now rival tribes of cognoscenti
Suppose the only truth is theirs.
Two rival shrines to one Old Master
Is either a PR disaster
Or one of Woland's later pranks
To sew confusion in the ranks
Of scholars, Goths and those still yearning
To bolt the stable door with locks
And demonstrate the Orthodox
Belief that books *are* made for burning.
Outside this evil little flat
We bump into a plump black cat.

ЭК

from The Worst Concoctions, vol.2

The Tale of a Dog

probably not by Viktor Pelyevin

Establishing shot. A bench outside a Metro station. Three men. One is taking photographs. One is studying a map. The third is anxiously watching a large black dog on the steps. They could be tourists, or part of a film-crew. Or spies. We do not know. The hand-held camera suggests they are being watched from the inside of a car. By other spies perhaps. The audience is complicit in the gaze of the voyeur. We are spying on the spies.

The dog bares its teeth, approaches the bench and lights a Belomor. The first man takes a photograph. The second is still looking at his map. The third man is clearly alarmed.

Close-up of the dog's face. On its collar is the name 'Sharik'. The dog is none other than the hero of Bulgakov's *The Heart of a Dog*, now an officer in the FSB. Incidentally, Sharik is a popular name in many African countries, meaning 'Child of God'. In English 'God' is an anagram of 'dog'. So Sharik is the backward child of a dog. The son of a bitch. And who was the biggest Son of a Bitch in modern Russian History?

Cut to 1940s footage of May Day in Red Square. Ranks of marching soldiers. Close-up of Stalin and Beria. Stalin bares his teeth and lights a Belomor.

Cut to the inside of a police-station. The three men are sitting at a plain table. They look worried. Tuz Buben, the legendary Moscow detective known in the force as 'Ace of Spades' snarls and points to the camera on the table in front of him. We cannot hear the conversation since we are watching behind a two-way mirror. He picks up the camera and impatiently flicks through its memory.

We are shown a rapid series of fuzzy images of station platforms and dogs sleeping outside Metro stations.

Buben throws the camera on the table and barks at a policeman by the door. The door opens. Colonel Sharik runs in and jumps on the table, wagging his ancient tail. He turns to the camera and growls, 'Total Security. When it comes to cameras, the Sony XLK9 is a Man's Best Friend. It's a dog-eat-dog world. Don't be a pussy.'

The dog winks. The three men start howling.

ЭК

The Wrist Watch

certainly not by Sergei Lukyanenko

I was lying on the steps outside Komsomolskaya station. It was late. The last commuters were making their way home, tired or drunk, or both.

Shapeshifters are not usually supposed to take animal form. But this was an emergency. Something was abroad, and threatening the precarious balance between the forces of Light and Darkness.

There was a serial killer on the Metro.

And he had to be stopped.

We normally leave this kind of thing to the Moscow Police Department. But this was different. The killer was one of the Eloi, the equivalent of Moscow's Golden Youth in our world. An untouchable caste of spoilt young aristos, the Eloi usually keep to their own kind, partying by night and sleeping by day, a situation that keeps both the Night Watch and the Day Watch happy.

But something had changed.

Ever since that crazy Orthodox sect went underground claiming that the world was about to end, the Night Watch had been expecting something to happen.

And now it had.

One of the Eloi had taken human form and was slaughtering the Morlocks, the creatures who live in the tunnels beneath the deepest levels of the city, who drive the trains, operate the escalators and clean the stations at night when the Metro isn't running. The millions of Muscovites who pass through the Metro each day never suspect that the illuminated M outside every station is the sign of the invisible Morlock-proletariat that keeps the system moving deep in their twilight catacombs.
I had been ordered to keep a look out among the sleeping dogs and shoeless drunks in Three Stations. The drunks didn't bother me. Nor did the other dogs. Some animals have always been sensitive to the presence of Others. Although it was cold in the square, the Metro station lit the pavement with a comforting, sleepy warmth. I was just falling asleep when I heard Sergei. He was sitting on the roof of the Kazan station, hooting wildly.

Sergei isn't a Shapeshifter. He really is an owl. Sergei usually hangs out at the Sverchkov Hotel in Kitai-Gorod. But that night he was my back-up. I pricked up my ears and tuned into the urgent message encoded in the owl's high-frequency screech.
I didn't have time to change into human form, so I entered the Twilight and bounded down the escalators. When I emerged I could smell the blood on the chandeliers. The platform was empty apart from three men. This far underground I couldn't make out their auras very clearly. They looked tired. For some reason they seemed familiar. Like characters I had once read about in a book.

One of the men had a strange hair-cut. Another was taking photographs. Of course it's against the rules to use cameras in the Metro, but no-one was going to stop him at this time of night. The third man had seen me. He didn't look too happy.

The men were staring at the Korin mosaics on the ceiling. Some of these (Nevsky, the Battle of Berlin) celebrate famous victories of the Night Watch. Others celebrate the triumphs of the Dark. Both sides argued over one of these mosaics for years, adding and subtracting the faces of their agents. The current version is supposed to represent a negotiated compromise. Of course it's a complete dog's breakfast. There are whole stations like this - Novokuznetskaya and Kievskaya for example - where you can trace the history of the negotiations on the walls. Three sheaves of corn or two T-34s for every dove of peace, and so on.

I felt the warm rush of Metro-wind on my coat. A train pulled into the station. The three men turned away from the mosaics and entered the train. No-one got out. The doors began closing. Almost too late, I realised there was something wrong. The driver. There wasn't one. It was one of the ghost-trains from Metro-2. The Day Watch sometimes use this line when they need to move about the city quickly, and without us knowing. A few years back there was a rumour going round about a haunted train on the Metro. So someone from the Day Watch put the story on the internet. After that, of course, everyone thought it was true, but no-one believed it.

The doors closed behind me. The carriage was empty. The three men were already asleep.

I heard a growl. We were not alone.

At the other end of the carriage was a wolf. A Tambov wolf.

The fur on my back stood on end. My tail was up. But I knew it was an unequal contest. There was no way I could call for help. I had walked into a trap.

There was only one chance. I had to waken the Magus. Barbarossa. Old red-beard himself, sleeping like Rip van Winkle in Red Square.

Before I could step into the Twilight the wolf leaped across the carriage, twisting in a bolt of silver flame as it began to shed its skins. The creature landed on its six legs, vast wings beating the air behind it.

It was the chief Archmage of the Day Watch.

A Dark Magician.

A Dark Magician of extraordinary power.

A Dark Magician with an extraordinary plan.

The monster laughed and a tornado wind raged around my ears. He laughed again and a bolt of lightning struck me in the chest. A Tsunami of blood swept through the train. The victory of the Darkness was almost complete. The world was about to end...

Unless.

My only hope was to find a *yurodivy*, a Fool or Holy Idiot. According to Jerome, the powers of Darkness have no jurisdiction over them. But the Archmage's powers were still growing at an exponential rate. It was almost too late. I had to find three *yurodivy*. But where could I find three complete idiots?

Just then the three men woke up. One yawned. One rubbed his eyes. One looked at his watch.

'Where are we?'

'I dunno.'

'Moscow?'

And the Archmage vanished in a cloud of dust.

ЭК

And This is Us

definitely not by Lev Rubenstein

1. This is us.

2. This is us again.

3. This is us outside the Metro.

4. And this is a dog, asleep.

5. Another dog, asleep.

6. And this is a drunk.

7. Sleeping like a dog outside the Metro.

8. Another drunk, also asleep.

9. This is a statue.

10. And this is another statue.

11. This is a dog and a drunk asleep by a statue.

12. This is a dog and a drunk. Asleep by a statue outside the Metro.

13. This is us with a dog and a drunk, asleep outside the Metro.

14. This is a statue of a dog.

15. This is the statue of a drunk.

16. This is us with a drunk by a statue of a dog.

17. This is us with a dog by a statue of a drunk.

18. This is us drunk with a dog by a statue, asleep outside the Metro.

19. This is us.

20. This is us.

21. This is us.

ЭК

Fabulous

A model of the Tatlin Tower
On Alla Pugacheva's roof
Reflects the hot spring sunset hour
That brings out Moscow's Golden Youth,
A race of guiltless, gilt Godivas
In 4x4s. Their wolfish drivers
Protect the flock of Bond-girl blondes
That comes to feed around the Ponds
Like species of exotic fauna.
The House of Lions is over there.
Old Krylov watches from the Square.
Outside the café on the corner
They serve Krylovsky borsch that's laced
With bits of tongue. A wicked taste.

ЭК

Partizanskaya I

'You cannot hang us all!' she shouted,
The noose around her neck. At least,
That's what the legend says, undoubted
For fifty years, but now policed
By those whose healthy paranoia
About the past extends to Zoya.
The days of Fadayev's *Young Guard*
Are gone for good. The young are hard
On ancient stories of Resistance.
As war-time generations fade
There's some suggest she was betrayed,
Or even question her existence.
But at her feet a coke-can holds
This spring of new-cut marigolds.

ЭК

Partizanskaya II

Partizanskaya got three platforms
to cope with Stalin's crowds of fans
for stadia which, like some artforms,
did not proceed past grandiose plans.
This open-stair, near-surface station,
its turnstiles placed so fare evasion
was easier than payment, saw
youths leap the banisters, ignore
their country's executed daughter
whose sculpture clutches rifled hope,
her throat defiant in the rope.
Its décor, pastoral crossed with slaughter:
drum magazines and creamy leaves
and *Shpagins* hanging from the trees.

Shpagin (Шпагин) — a machine gun devised by Alexei Shpagin
for use in wintry conditions in the Great Patriotic War, also
known as the PPSh 41 or Burp Gun.

BHX

Vernissazh

Browse Vernissazh, half-built, half-broken,
view its mocked-up muck-spangled domes;
buy fake-fur *shapkas*, metro tokens,
old stamps, false ikons; ransack homes
for ration books and Tsarist roubles –
or slip next door, to where its double
spreads veg and duvets in the dirt
and gangsters sell you back your shirt.
The widest hucksters sell the mildest
products out – slippers, kettles, caps
(two followed us, like helpful chaps).
Here we lost Andy to the wildest
of worries, twitching at the bar
while he bought pressies in *Stab'im Pazaar*...

shapka (шапка) — characteristic Russian fur cap with ear-flaps.

BHX

Call Me Izmaylovksy Park

Naw, creh me ut, like waukendreme
wiz some auld air thon carriage kent,
a metro emergin fae thi deeps
tae meet ghaist riders i thi trees –

hussars fae some fecht lang forgot
e'en beh thir mithers, thir ain souls
lang-coosht in thi lift's far langer moniplies,
hauf-digestit beh thir God.

But aa thi warkirs, comin hame,
saw sabers cut and cannons blaw,
and tripes o riders trip thir ain
cuddies – wan, heid chappt in twa

beh pikestaff, splay-hoofed thi platform –
aabdy hauf-rehsin as thi doors
slammed on thon steed, skliddrin in uts ain
bluid, hauf-enterin thi train

and bein split, spilt coils o green
entrails lashin thi flair,
gress spluttirt on thi shoon
o onywan that wad pairt

dwaum fae darg, or aiblins hud
lang learnt tae, that here were caad
tae witness Mither Russ
regurgitate her ain weans' bluid.

creh — cry, call by name; *waukendreme* — hallucination; *haill* — whole; *ghaist* — ghost; *i* — in; *beh* — by; *coosht* — embraced; *lift* — heavens; *moniplies* — intestines; *warkirs* — workers; *hame* — home; *ain* — own; *cuddies* — horses; *chappt* — chopped; *aabdy* — everybody; *rehsin* — rising; *skliddrin* — slipping; *dwaum* — dream; *darg* — a day's labour; *caad* — called; *weans* — children; *bluid* — blood.

BHX

gossamer

spellbound again. the slow glide
of her measured stride, each low-
heeled footfall incising a wound
through the flushing flesh of rush-
hour huddles. miss armenia's eyes
are bowed, her knitted skirt &
chocolate tights are gripping her
curves like the weight of drizzle.

& then to us, *brodyagi*; our gossamer
words sinking in the marsh, our thoughts
wandering like a clan of cursed jews.
last night i dreamed of krylov's dogs
dagger-tongued & bitter of spleen,
stripping the bones of my rhetoric bare.

ПС

The Golden Fork

Though my story is not true,
'Tis a lesson, lads, to you.
(Pushkin)

They had a competition
to pick a cosmodog
(not mentioning the mission
was to boil up like a frog).

From Beloruss came Belka
while Laika came from Lem,
from Stranraer Toon came Strelka –
or maybe that was Perm.

They set those mutts a problem
'This *shashlik's* stacked with pork,
but if you wish to gobble'im
you must find the Golden Fork…'

(How vulgar is this fable?
Hounds are innocent at heart –
we'd all be, were we able
to lick our private parts.)

'…each golden tine is skewered
with three million cobs of corn:
while the Motherland is poorer
than a thumb upon a thorn.'

The night was like a mitten
some *zek* dropped on the road,
three-fingered, as though knitten
for the grandson of a toad.

The pointer took the digit
while Laika tracked the thumb,
the lapdog had a fidget
and then she dragged her bum.

First Belka felt a bee-sting
and then she heard a gong,
and knew this was the precinct
of the Sheriff of Hong Kong.

First Laika saw the lightning
then the thunder deigned to crash,
then she knew this was the frightening
Factory of Gnash.

Meanwhile Strelka had a weewee,
then she had a sleep,
selecting where some seaweed
had made a stinky heap.

The decadent old palace
in which the Sheriff dwelled
was flaking like a callus
and all his chopsticks smelt.

The production line of dentures
was grinning like a chimp
but Laika's bold adventure
felt like a leek gone limp.

Both canines caned it backwards
to where old Strelka slept –
it's here where humans lack words
that the nose grows more adept.

That fork (lost by a mermaid,
who'd used it in her hair)
from beneath the hound from Perm said,
'I'll claw you like a bear!'

– Though this was more a fragrance
which only Laika traced,
for which they made this vagrant
first of dogs in space!

shashlik (шашлык) — kebab; *zek* (зак, short for *zaklyuchonniy*,
заключенный) —prisoner.

BHX

Slava to the Metro

Slava to the Metro now it's passed its Biblical span!
I celebrate your seventy-somethingth naked before
North Shields – Severniyeshitskaya in the slush –
its paltry echo of your buried mock-frog temples,
a lapel badge's *Ehm* driven through my foreskin,
a breakfast street beer in my plastered fist,
much like the *spekulyanti* outside Semyonovskaya,
much like the dogs asleep in the unexpected sunlight,
much like the stubby finger of the indicating titan
plaster-of-partisans in the *pasazh* between
the two stations of Belorusskaya, much slenderer in
the old photographs, less clumsily-replaced, less caressed.
Slava! with its conglomerative connotations
of Slav and slave and lava, the three forces that would seem
to have combined to work your seams
and hollow out your tunnels, ghosts of the naked children
drowned at Komsomolskaya still glimpsed from the platform
transparent as squid in the tunnels' depths,
heat of those depths still rising to wrap the splayed man
trembling in his slumbers outside Chistiye Prudi, his
shapka's attic cheekflaps battened down for the night.
Slava! to your attributes of rubber steel and formica,
glaucoma globes on stalks, stubby batons of light
down the centres of loam-dark escalators,
your marbles tiles and brasses, among the dead
airmen brought to earth, mere boys with model planes,
pilots so far below their contrails as though the dead
could fall upwards through the earth, shrouds for
parachutes, towards the resurrection of each Easter,
each May Day, helpless in your eruptive rhetoric.

Slava! as you were born in contractions of the clay,
epidural freezings, as you were brought up
to be blinded by the flags, waving in the hot breath
of tunnels, patriotic tubercules, as you matured
to the dead celebrated everywhere, scarcely out of school
before uniformly tumbled in the pit of brothers,
as you *sobornost*-ed up, stagnified, joined in the pogrom
of the icons, their dead moustaches sweeping the platforms clear
each latest late leader ineluctably unelectable,
so you could age but never fail, each vein, chamber, artery
still thronged as you attempt a second life: *slava! slava! slava!*

slava (слава) – hail/glory to; *Ehm* — the Russian letter 'M' (also 'I
am' in Dundonian Scots); *spekulyanti* (спекулянты) — illegal
traders; *pasazh* (пассаж) — passage; *sobornost* (соборность) —
spiritual community

BHX

Against the Fingers of the Clock

'Earphones, earphones' (Mandelstam)

At night the Circle Line goes round,
Three hundred feet below the ground,
De-dum de-dum, de-dum de-dum –
The evening rhythm has become
The patter of iambic feet,
A rising, falling, even beat;
'Dear Passengers, Dear Passengers'
The woman on the tannoy purrs,
Which means we're going widdershins
Against the circle as it spins,
Or else that we are going home.
This soporific metronome
s' the back-beat to the sleepy mime
Of those now travelling back in time:
A young man strokes his girlfriend's hair,
Old women move their lips in prayer,
A small boy grips his father's coat,
A mobile bleeps its sputnik note,
A baby sleeps, two lovers kiss,
And far away the iPods hiss
Their susurrus of faint applause
Like waves upon the silent shores
Of midnight islands far away,
A lullaby that seems to say,
All Moscow girls are beautiful
All Moscow girls are beautiful…

protiv chasovoy strelkiy (против часовой стрелки) — anti-
clockwise (against the fingers of the clock); *sputnik* (спутник) —
a travelling companion; also the name of the first
communications satellite launched by the Soviet Union in 1957.

ЭК

three toasts

to the humanist, the rationalist,
the third internationalist, their
treatise on superstition revised;
who stroked a chutzpah hound for
luck, even themselves surprised
by the magnet pull of its polished cock.

to all those modern serfs who surf
this continuum of the bearable
to those who still believe the lie
that our pasts remain repairable
to those who find a kind of hope
in the words of that meek parable

to the swan, the crayfish & the pike
who despite received opinion are all alike.

ПС

The Song of the Tourists

*Some people say there is nothing better than the Taj Mahal, but I know they
are wrong, In the Moscow Metro there's a Taj Mahal at each station.*
(Alexander Khaletski)

We didn't take the Kremlin tour,
  We missed the Moscow Ballet,
We didn't see the Tatlin Tower,
  The Bolshoi or the Maly;
Our schedule was so busy that
  It didn't leave us room
To say a prayer at Yeltsin's grave
  Or queue for Lenin's tomb;
St Basil's Church was out of bounds,
  (Though not for bad behaviour)
We didn't climb the Lenin Hills
  Or swim in Christ the Saviour;
The Tretyakov Museum alas
  Just wasn't on our list,
The Palace of the Soviets
  For us did not exist;
We didn't shop in GUM or TsUM
  Or buy a Russian bride,
We didn't stroll down Gorky Street
  To be taken for a ride;
We didn't smuggle nuclear waste
  For men with soulless eyes,
We weren't picked up in Gorky Park
  Accused of being spies;
We didn't see the Future work
  Or meet a billionaire,
We didn't sleep beneath the stars
  In old Three Stations Square...

But the tourists on the train went round and round,
Round and round, round and round,
Yes the tourists on the train went round and round,
All day long.

(Repeat)

ЭК

departures

& out of your suffering
we will build mammon.

i try in vain to coax a smile
from the faces of the dead.

garlands for the glorious,
conspicuous & victorious,

each faded tessari petal
the colour of a frozen tear.

this city is a conical adrift
left spinning on the marsh.

today, i see home in the face
of every child, these idle

arms yearning for the dead-
weight of my sleeping boys.

ПC

Epilogue: Fellow Travellers

No other railway in the world has ever had so many owners.
(Bertolt Brecht)

Dem bones, dem bones gonna walk aroun' until the break of day.
(Traditional)

The system's closing down; it's almost one.
   Escaping from the sleepless night above us
We join the usual cast of sleepy lovers,
   Of night-shift workers, students, porters, punks,
The bomzh and bums and shoeless cobbler-drunks
   Now counting crows, the blind drunk and the blind,
The Moscow girls who leave the West behind,
   Pale, fur-lined Olga Kurylenko clones
With chilling Snow Queen eyes and frozen bones
   Like skeletons beneath their perfect skin.
Their priceless beauty's only rouble-thin.
   The Metro graveyard shift is clocking on.

Here myth and magic mix with the mundane.
   Before the last train out tonight departs
Sretenskiy Bul'var, the night-shift starts
   To sweep the midnight Metro catacombs,
A regiment of witches with their brooms.
   A Bilibin-like babushka stands facing
The question, 'Russia, whither art thou racing?'
   (*Dead Souls* Part I) inscribed upon the wall.
She gives no answers, though she's heard them all.
   She's seen the future and it works long hours.
The present is a bunch of crumpled flowers
   And History is a drunk who's missed the train.

Down here among these bruised and bottled boozers
    It's said that you can sometimes hear the squeals
Of suicides beneath the carriage wheels
    Of empty, midnight trains that have no drivers;
Perhaps it's just the ghosts of crash survivors,
    Or maybe it's the sound of Metro-2
(The ghostly system built for you know who).
    But tales of Metro spirits fill the void
When other kinds of faith have been destroyed,
    And maybe when you're heading home to bed
It's hard to tell the dead drunk from the dead,
    The legless and the lost from History's losers.

Once caught inside the Metro's spider pattern,
    We weave our way round webs of urban myth
Re-told by Lukyanenko and Cruz-Smith,
    Moskva-Petushki meets *The Twilight Zone.*
Some say the Metro's coughing up its bones
    (*Ezekiel* 37) between the tracks –
The soft and matted curses of the zeks,
    The wet dreams of the Komsomols who drowned,
The cries of orphans buried underground,
    The laughter of the architects whose faint
Designs still show beneath the fading paint.
    October's children swallowed whole by Saturn.

Among the ghosts who've joined us for the ride
    Is one old Durham miner called George Short.
Black-listed after '26, George fought
    Against the Means-Test, organised the ban
On Teesside pig-iron destined for Japan
    In '38; he led the local fight
Against the Blackshirts, won the public's right
    To speak at Stockton Cross (for which he spent
Three months in gaol); and when the Party sent
    Him here for cadre-training, volunteered
To dig these Metro tunnels. So I'm cheered
    To feel his rebel spirit at our side.

For comrades such as George the age was drawn
    In simple black and white chiaroscuro.
He was a cartoon Tankie to my Euro,
    A hard-line Old Believer, unimpressed
By voices through the Smoke of Budapest,
    As if the laws of change do not apply
To change itself. And yet I can't deny
    That some of those whom I have most admired
Themselves admired the will that was required
    To change the world and bring to bloody birth
Inside these marvelled halls beneath the earth
    A painful future struggling to be born.

This 'Metro' comes from *metra* (Greek for womb),
    The kind of joke that Platonov enjoyed,
And so from *Happy Moscow* straight to Freud:
    The rational city blinking in the light
That keeps its deepest secrets out of sight;
    The Ego-Eloi who don't want to know
The Morlock-Id who really runs the show
    (Why else are labour's efforts called the *base*?)
As propaganda is the human face
    By which all states declare they will prevail,
So here inside the rib-cage of the whale
    All questions are reduced to who and whom.

These images of endless cornucopia
    Suggest the good intentions of the State,
Like decorations round an empty plate;
    A dream of Holy Rus or old Cockaigne,
From which now only crumbs of hope remain.
    The World Turned Upside Down's turned inside out
Belief is just another word for doubt,
    And History is a dog that's lost its balls.
The fields of golden wheat-sheaves on the walls
    Stand like abundant metonyms for famine,
Ironic harvest halls which we examine
    As if each grain of truth contains dystopia.

The builders of the Metro understood
     This railway is a system of belief
Confessed in marble, gilt and bas-relief.
     It's four-fifths engineering, one fifth art,
But where does one part end, the other start?
     Down here of course the deepest structure's binary:
Utile/dulce, hand/brain, function/finery,
     The realms of darkness/light, above/below,
A bread and circus horror show, as though
     The Base and Superstructure paradigm
Goes deeper than geology and time,
     Like seams of coal contained within the wood.

We mummify the future in the past
     And hope that something good will one day grow,
Like Russian spuds beneath the winter snow.
     Apocalyptic sects go underground
As though the word of God sounds more profound
     In amniotic caves of dark and dread.
Like Comrade Mole we crawl among the dead;
     Like shadows on the wall of Plato's cave;
Or like Persephone, whose winter grave
     Was premised on the faith that it would bring
The pomegranate promise of the Spring –
     And hope the next one's better than the last.

It's nearly time for us to disappear;
     First thing tomorrow morning we're off home,
Still clutching our old volumes of Jerome
     As if they made a map through History's maze
(*cf* the Vernissazh on busy days),
     A *Rough Guide* to the Metro of the mind.
As if on cue, on our last night we find
     They're showing on some Russian tv station
The classic 70's Soviet adaptation
     Of *Three Men in a Boat* (plus *dance* routines).
Though we were here, don't ask us what it means –
     We barely dipped our whiskers in the beer.

ЭК   115

Notes

Metronomic
There is a legend that the Circle line follows the mark left by Stalin's coffee cup on the blueprints.

The Dog's Bollocks
There are seventy-six groups of sculptures on the platform of Ploshad' Revolyutsiy station, each design appearing twice.

TsUm
Moscow's first department store (*Tsentralniy Universalniy Magazin*, or 'Central Department Store') was built in 1908 by the Scottish firm Muir & Mirrielees, after whom Chekhov did indeed name his dogs.

Mayakovskaya
Mayakovskaya Metro station includes thirty-four ceiling mosaics depicting the '24-hour Soviet Sky'. They were made by Vladimir Frolov from the designs of Alexander Deyneka and airlifted to Moscow during the siege of Leningrad. The ceiling of the new exit from the station features several lines from Mayakovsky's 'Moscow Sky'.

Borovitskaya
At the entrance to the Metro station is the inscription 'We Are Your Children, Moscow', also the title of an autobiography by Moscow Mayor Yuri Luzhkov.

Belichniy Gory
Squirrel Hills is a non-existent metro station in the Zabarabashkareche district, designed by Alexei Bezyzvestnykh in 1991.

Taganskaya
The Metro station, which was opened in 1966, is decorated with images of balloonists, pilots, sputniks, cosmonauts - and Icarus. Five years earlier, the Soviet cosmonaut Yuri Gagarin became the

first human to travel into space, and the first to observe that the Earth is blue.

Tsaritsino

The Love Ball at Tsaritsino Park in February 2008 was an attempt to revive the charity balls of Imperial Russia. The auction - which raised $6m for the children's charity the Naked Heart Foundation - included a tuxedo hand-tailored by Giorgio Armani (110,000 euros), a Valentino wedding-dress (600,000 euros), a selection of rare vintages from Chateau Lafite Rothschild (160,000 euros) and a Damien Hirst painting (1.2 million euros). An estimated 2 million children live on the street in Russia. *Nasha Rasha* is a popular comedy on Russian television.

Chkhalovskaya

This station opened in 1995 on the Lyublinskaya line, and was named after the Soviet aviator Valery Chkalov, who flew several long-distance flight in the mid-thirties, including a flight over the North Pole, before dying in 1938 whilst test-flying a prototype aircraft.

Rimskaya

The plaques and statues were made by the sculptor Leonid Berlin. The station was also opened in 1995.

Novodevichiy

The cemetery at Novodevichiy Convent contains the remains of many of Russia's most famous politicians, artists, composers and writers, including Gogol, whose coffin was famously opened to find scratch-marks on the lid, indicating he had been buried alive. 'Le Poete Allongé' is a poem by Paul Durcan about falling asleep on the Moscow Metro.

Komsomolskaya

The entrance to Komsomolskaya station is on Komsomolskaya Square, also known as Three Station Square because of the proximity of the Leningrad, Yaroslav and Kazan railway stations.

The square is home to many of the city's homeless.

Ode: re Spartak FC
OMON, FSB, the Militsiya are various wings of the Russian security forces. OMON are a paramilitary unit on riot control and counter-iterrrorism duties, and the FSB are effectively the successors to the KGB. The Militsiya are regular police, often on duty in Metro stations.

VDNKh
Lysenko was Stalin's favourite geneticist. Nashi is the youth-wing of the ruling United Russia party.

Stalker
A 1979 film by the director Andrei Tarkovsky, in which three characters attempt to access a chamber located in the centre of the Zone, a devastated landscape.

To Say Nothing of the Dog
Mendeleevskaya station is named after the Russian chemist Dmitri Mendeleev, creator of the periodic table (and father-in-law of the poet Alexandr Blok). In 2007 a bronze monument to stray dogs was installed in the station in memory of Malchik, a favourite dog of passengers and metro workers at the station. The subscription committee which raised the money for the statue included the poets Bella Akhmadulina and Fasil Iskander. The statue was unveiled on the last day of the Year of the Dog.

Laika
Laika (meaning 'Howler') became the first creature to orbit the Earth in 1957 on board Sputnik 2. She died within hours of takeoff due to a malfunction in the life support system, but encouraged Soviet scientists to believe that manned space flights were possible.

Oktyabrskaya
Designed by Leonid Polyakov in 1950, the main hall has, at its far end, an empty apse behind a locked grille, intended to represent

both sunlight and a radiant future. People often agree to meet 'under the sky at Oktyabrskaya.'

May Day
The statue of Karl Marx still stands in Teatralnaya Square. Dzerzhinky Square is now Lubyanka Square, the site of a memorial to the victims of the Gulag. Felix Dzershinksy founded the Cheka.

Pegasus' Stables
The Bulgakov House and the rival Bulgakov Foundation are both in the apartments where Bulgakov lived on Bolshaya Sadova. Woland is the name of the devil in Bulgakov's *The Master and Margarita*. In 2006 the stairwell of the building was damaged by a member of the Orthodox Church who claimed to be resisting 'satanic propaganda'.

Fabulous
The Master and Margarita begins at the Patriarch Ponds. Alla Pugacheva is a famous Russian pop-singer; the Lion House used to be the residence of Soviet military leaders; Ivan Krylov was a nineteenth-century Russian satirist and writer of animal fables.

Partizanskaya
Zoya Kosmodemyanskaya was a young Komsomol member executed by the Nazis outside Moscow in 1941.There is a statue in her memory at the recently re-named Partizanskaya Metro station. Alexander Fadayev's novel about young partisans, *Young Guard* was published in 1946. The Russian Orthodox Church is currently considering her canonisation.

Vernissazh
A mock-medieval construction (also known as Izmaylovo Market), this sells all kinds of souvenirs, memorabilia and tat to tourists. It adjoins a standard market selling more useful goods to Muscovites.

Fellow Travellers

The actress Olga Kurylenko (*Quantum of Solace*) was spotted by a model-scout on the Moscow Metro when she was just thirteen. Ivan Bilibin was a Soviet artist famous for illustrating Russian folk-tales. Venedikt Erofyeev's novel *Moskva-Petushki* records a drunken train-journey from Moscow. In Andrei Platanov's novel *Happy Moscow* the eponymous heroine volunteers to help build the first line of the Metro.

The contributors

Andy Croft's books include *Red Letter Days, Out of the Old Earth, Selected Poems of Randall Swingler, A Weapon in the Struggle* and *Comrade Heart*. He has written forty non-fiction books (mostly about football) and three novels for teenagers. Writing Residencies include the Great North Run, the Hartlepool Headland, the Southwell Poetry Festival and HMP Holme House. His books of poetry include *Nowhere Special, Gaps Between Hills, Headland, Just as Blue, Great North, Comrade Laughter, Ghost Writer* and *Sticky*. He has edited the anthologies *Holme and Away, Speaking English, Red Sky at Night* (with Adrian Mitchell), *North by North East* (with Cynthia Fuller) and *Not Just a Game* (with Sue Dymoke). He lives in Middlesbrough.

W.N. Herbert has published seven volumes of poetry, including *The Testament of the Reverend Thomas Dick, The Laurelude, Cabaret McGonagall* (short-listed for the Forward Prize), *The Big Bumper Book of Troy, Forked Tongue* and *Bad Shaman Blues* (both short-listed for the T.S. Eliot Prize). His poetry is widely anthologised. Other books include a study of the Scots poet Hugh MacDiarmid, *To Circumjack MacDiarmid*, the bestselling anthology *Strong Words: modern poets on modern poetry* (edited with Matthew Hollis) and *A Balkan Exchange: Eight Bulgarian and British Poets*. He is Professor of Poetry and Creative Writing in the School of English at Newcastle University.

Paul Summers' poetry publications include *Vermeer's Dark Parlour, Beer & Skittles, The Last Bus, The Rat's Mirror, Cunawabi* and *Big Bella's Dirty Café*. He was founding co-editor of the magazines *Billy Liar* and *Liar Republic* and a co-director of Liar Inc, facilitating creative projects across the North of England in educational and community contexts. He has also written for TV, film, radio and theatre and has collaborated many times with artists on mixed-media projects, most recently *Home (in 3 bits)*, a spoken word/music collaboration with musician Dave Hull-Denholm. He lives in North Shields.